MW01089538

ISBN-13 978-0-9914230-5-7

Library of Congress Control Number: 2017952142

www.angiesplace.org

Hi, my name's Courage! What's yours?
Dr. Vauthy

My **friends** are here to share their **stories with you** about their adventures in **Angie's Place.**
PUPP
BENTLEY

HEATER
Angie's Place is a children's library named after a little girl with an illness called Cystic Fibrosis who loved books.
It's a place to make friends!
The Angela Liden Library
founded by Alliene and Dick Liden
It's a place to laugh or cry till your sides hurt, like mine!
Band-Aid, please.

This is where medicine for the **spirit** is found, to **help** you while you're **in the hospital**.
angie's place
A HEALING STORY
The **doctor and nurses** have medicine for your body, but **this** is for your **spirit**.
What gives you **joy**?
uhm...

Come on.
Pick a **book**.
Read it and use the **art** as a way to **guide your imagination.**
Or if you like to **read with your ears,** pick out an **audio** book. You could also explore a **website** on the computer.
There are **adventure programs** like **puppet theatre!** In the **Paws Program** you read to **dogs!**
There's **Story Time** and guest author visits.
Even the **zoo** brings **live animals** for a school program!
Other times, something an animal might leave **behind,** like a **snakeskin!**

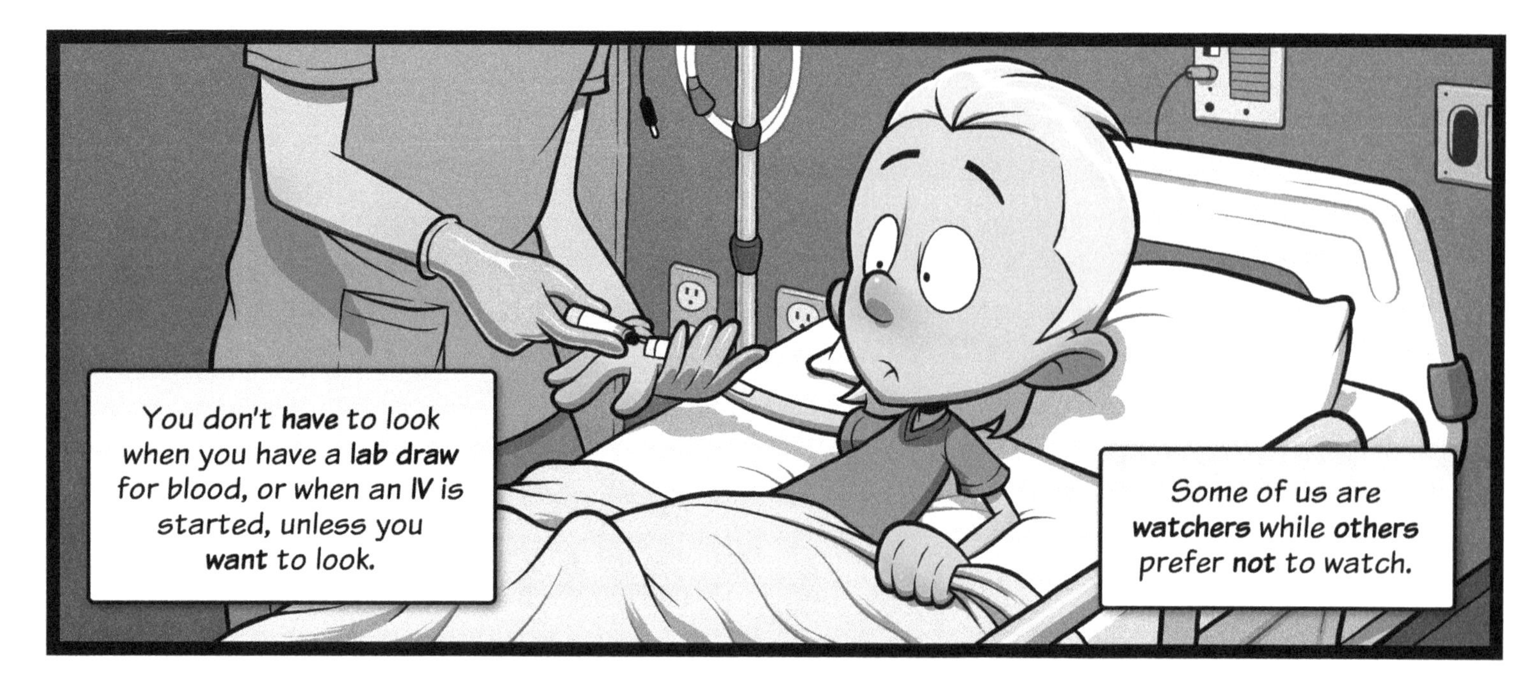
You don't **have** to look when you have a **lab draw** for blood, or when an **IV** is started, unless you **want** to look.
Some of us are **watchers** while **others** prefer **not** to watch.

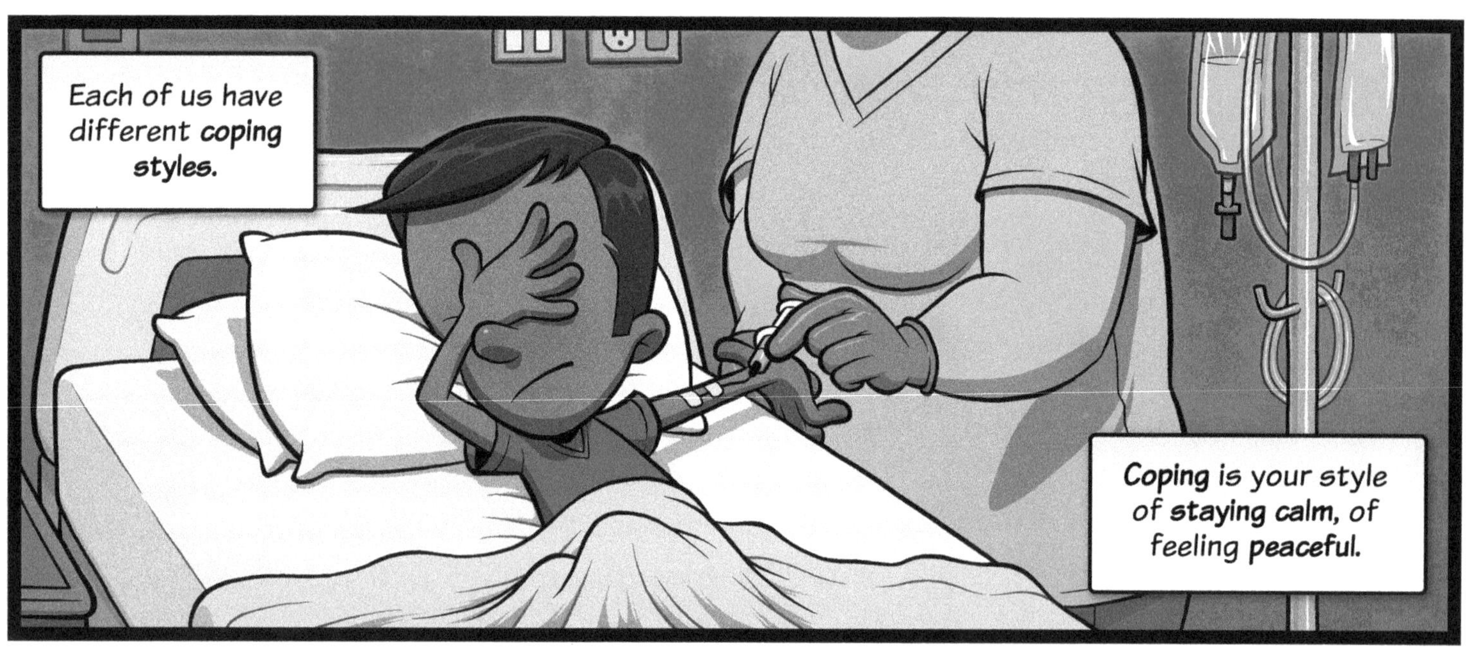
Each of us have different **coping styles.**
Coping is your style of **staying calm**, of feeling **peaceful.**

Some of us like a good **story.**
Good **stories** are found in good **books,** and you get **those** at **the library!**

I'm learning how to take my medicine, it's a funny name "in sul in" with my play nurses kit. Mommy gives me my medicine after poking my finger to see how much I need and I pretend with my doll to give her medicine too to keep her strong. My big brother shows me pictures in my books and reads to me after my medicine because I'm a big girl when I take my medicine--it makes mommy smile.

If you **don't** want to look, **here's** an idea: it's called **diversion.**
Keep your **mind** away from **this moment.**
Have someone hold a **book** in **front of** the medical procedure so you don't **see** what is **happening.**
Remember, it's **your choice.** You can read **out loud** or have your **parent** read so **others can share** in it.
6
Before you **know** it, it's **over** and it was not such a **bad experience.**
The **bonus** is: you learned **interesting facts** about something you **love,** like **dolphins, race cars,** or **fairies...**
...so while your **spirit** soars, so does your **intelligence.**

If you like to listen, put an audio book in a CD player to hear a narrator make the story exciting with their voice!
Some of these audio books have music or sound effects to increase the believability!
Sometimes medicine makes it hard to focus and audio books help you relax.
Anyway, that's what Peter says. Peter was born blind.
WHALES
When he's not reading his braille books, he's listening to audio books and says it transports him into other worlds.
This is Jamecia singing!
Before this, she didn't say a word to anyone for two days. This song reminded her of a song at her preschool - bringing her a happy memory.
She has been so sick with pneumonia that it hurt when she breathed.

Consider flashlight reading.
Darken the room, illuminate each word, and give yourself time to sound each word.
Pretend like you are a Halloween character while reading and imitate the voice of your favorite character.

My name is Jonathan. The car accident scared me so much but I'm relaxing with this audio book with soothing music background to keep my mind off the accident. My grandpa is next to me comforting me and trying to make jokes. Listening to ocean sounds and an adventure story reminds us of family vacations at the beach. This helps!

You love animals, and right now you are especially missing your best animal friend, who is at home.
Then you are invited to a special program to meet a dog in the library.
In the Paws Program, you know you're telling a good story when a tail starts wagging!
On other days there is Max, who is a gentle boxer who likes to have his belly rubbed.
Everyone knows how hard it is to take medicine. You don't have a choice with your medicine and medical tests, but when you are in the library you get to make the choices.

If you pretend to sneeze, Penny runs for a Kleenex box, pulls one out and races to give one to you.
BENTLEY
Watch out for Bentley! He is a huge Irish Wolfhound, but so gentle.
He has his very own trampoline at home. Wolfhounds don't live much longer than six years because of their genetics and knowing how short their life span is reminds us to cherish every day.
When you visit the dogs, your blood pressure improves. You are calmer when petting them. When you are visiting with other kids, you are not so lonely.
Before you know it, you don't feel sad about being away from your pets anymore, because you've made new friends!

The **dogs** get **blood tests,** just like you.
They also go to a **dog school** to learn to be **calm** around **hospital** sounds like the **beep, beep, beep** of an IV pump.
If a child **cries,** or **squeals,** or the **IV pump** starts to **beep,** they stay very still.
BENTLEY

“My name is Roberto and I have asthma. It's a reactive airway disease which means I struggle to breathe when there is a trigger--like dust mites, or animal fur... but when hypoallergenic dogs visit like a Portuguese water dog or poodle then I'm able to join the fun too!

I always keep my inhaler by my side. It releases a tiny spray of medicine that helps me breathe. The medicine is in aerosol form, and gets drawn into my lungs by inhaling deeply and then holding my breath for ten seconds. A lot of star athletes have asthma, but they won't let it get in the way of championship rings or gold medals!”

Biofacts come from animals, like the shell a snail leaves behind, or a lost bird feather.
A shark tooth is also a biofact.
The Zoo Director was our guest Story Time reader in Angie's Place.
PUPPET THEATER
We had puppets for the reading of a story about a little boy who helps save Leopold's home because the glaciers are melting (Leopold is a polar bear and the name of Angie's great-grandfather).
Pop quiz: do polar bears come from the north or south pole?

After reading about Leopold, this book was dedicated to Angie's Place.
How exciting! Your photo may appear in the newspaper, too!
The news media comes sometimes. With your parent's permission, you might be able to be on TV!
After Story Time, the Zoo teacher provides a program with biofacts like penguin skins.
Did you know a penguin skin is actually made up of tiny feathers?
They let you touch the things they bring in, then you wash your hands. They also brought tiger and cheetah skins, and a polar bear foot!
But just wait until you hear about the "live" animals!

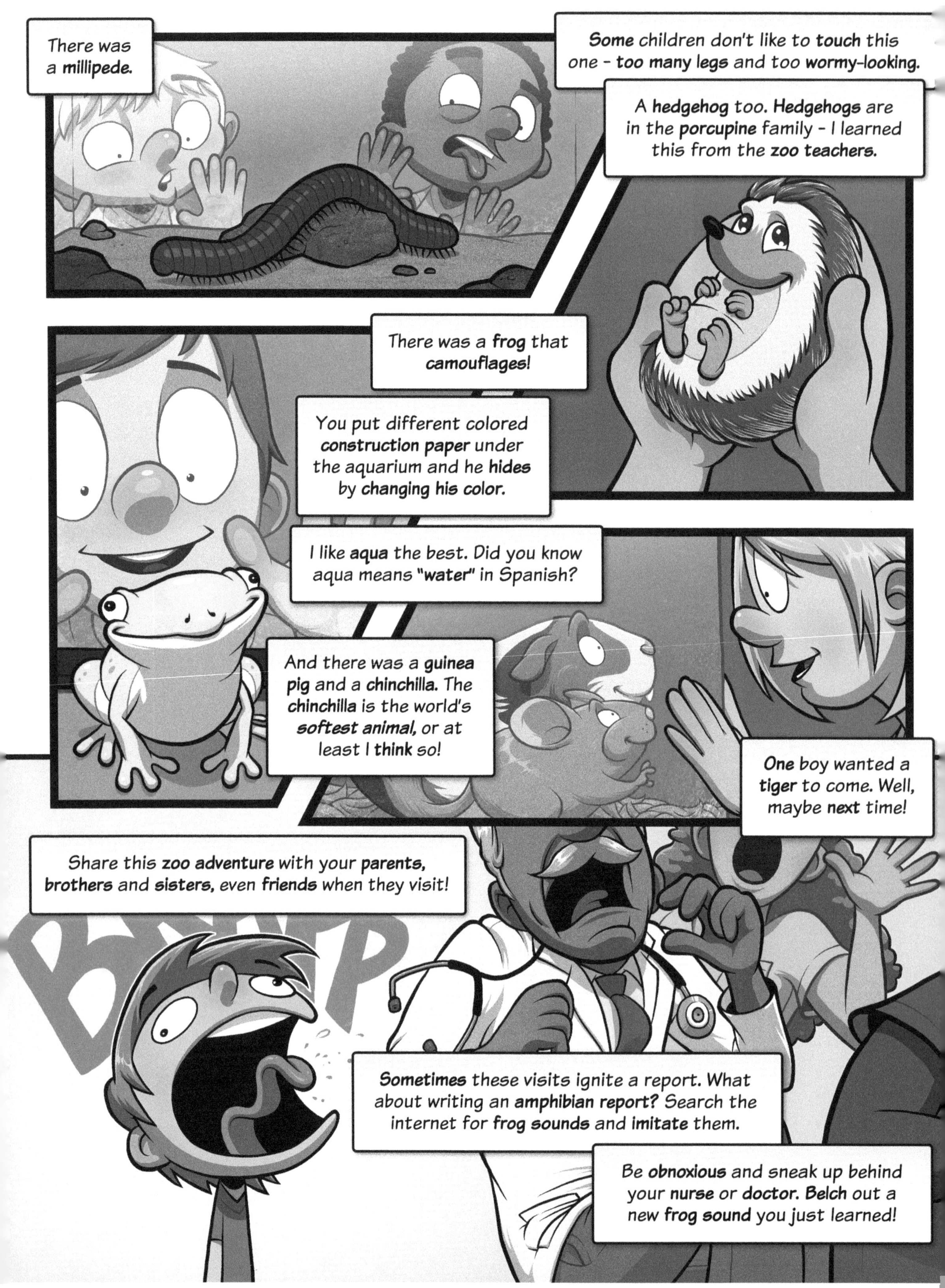
There was a millipede.
Some children don't like to touch this one - too many legs and too wormy-looking.
A hedgehog too. Hedgehogs are in the porcupine family - I learned this from the zoo teachers.
There was a frog that camouflages!
You put different colored construction paper under the aquarium and he hides by changing his color.
I like aqua the best. Did you know aqua means "water" in Spanish?
And there was a guinea pig and a chinchilla. The chinchilla is the world's softest animal, or at least I think so!
One boy wanted a tiger to come. Well, maybe next time!
Share this zoo adventure with your parents, brothers and sisters, even friends when they visit!
BURP
Sometimes these visits ignite a report. What about writing an amphibian report? Search the internet for frog sounds and imitate them.
Be obnoxious and sneak up behind your nurse or doctor. Belch out a new frog sound you just learned!

The rule for school work is: only do it if it relaxes you while you're in the hospital.
Remember, your goal is to reduce stress. Not increase it.
If you come out of your room, with an okay from the nurse or doctor, then go to the children's library.
What are you waiting for? The library has dictionaries, encyclopedias, software, computers and literature as a choice - not a punishment - so enjoy!
But don't get monkey hairs in the computers - it really slows them down!
With the internet on the computers, you can complete your homework or get your assignments online.
If you cannot leave your room, ask for a portable computer. This can be set up near your bed for comfort.
What's your favorite subject? Is it History? Poetry, maybe?
Ask your parent, a friend or a family member to bring in your school work.

If it's a **difficult** subject (otherwise known as a "no, **anything** but **that**" subject) - like **math**, for example - you might get **frustrated.**
Ask a **friend** to **sit** with you and **help you** by giving you **special attention.**
Time will **fly** when you're searching the **internet,** listening to an **audiobook,** or enjoying a **puppet performance.** You've heard about **flying time,** right?
You can **even** put on your **own** puppet show!
Some cameras record **video** so you can make your **own personal movie!**
Grab a pencil and sketch whatever pops into your **head!** There are also **How-To** books that teach you **how to draw!**

"I'm Holly. Because I used drugs, I've been in trouble with my parents, at school and with the cops. I had to go into a special unit in the hospital called Behavior Medicine to learn how to change, where they teach you through therapy groups and with books to learn how to quit. This helped save my life I'm grateful for the insight about how to boost my self-esteem and to make decisions using healthy values.

After I leave here I'll continue to go for counseling and be given more assignments. I know it will take time, but I want my life back, and I'm determined. These books have helped change my thinking already, and I respect myself now."

The library has educational videos for you to check out about fossils, rivers, oceans, horses, climate...
Become an expert: read a magic book.
You're in the hospital. You have time to practice your tricks: set up a time to perform with an audience if you can leave your room.
No wonder my ears are so long!
MAGIC
If you can't leave your room, practice on the medical team, the doctors, nurses, lab techs, visitors...

Origami is a great way to pass the day!
You should practice it carefully.
I get all mixed up when I try it, but that's just me!

We had dancers from a studio perform in the hospital and bring a book to life.
While the book Color Dance was read out loud, the dancers used colored scarves to mix colors.
Librarians and guest authors make appearances. Sometimes they bring CDs to sing along with the story you've just read together.
You can even make up your own creative ending to a story!

If you're a teen, you know this Story Time is too young for you, but humor yourself and go watch the expressions of disbelief!
If you can't leave your room to go to Angie's Place Library because of a fever, for example...
...or if you don't feel well enough to leave your room, the library will come to you.
When you share a story together you feel closer as a family.
Lean back in your bed and look at the images in the book to help soothe you. Colors can help you heal.

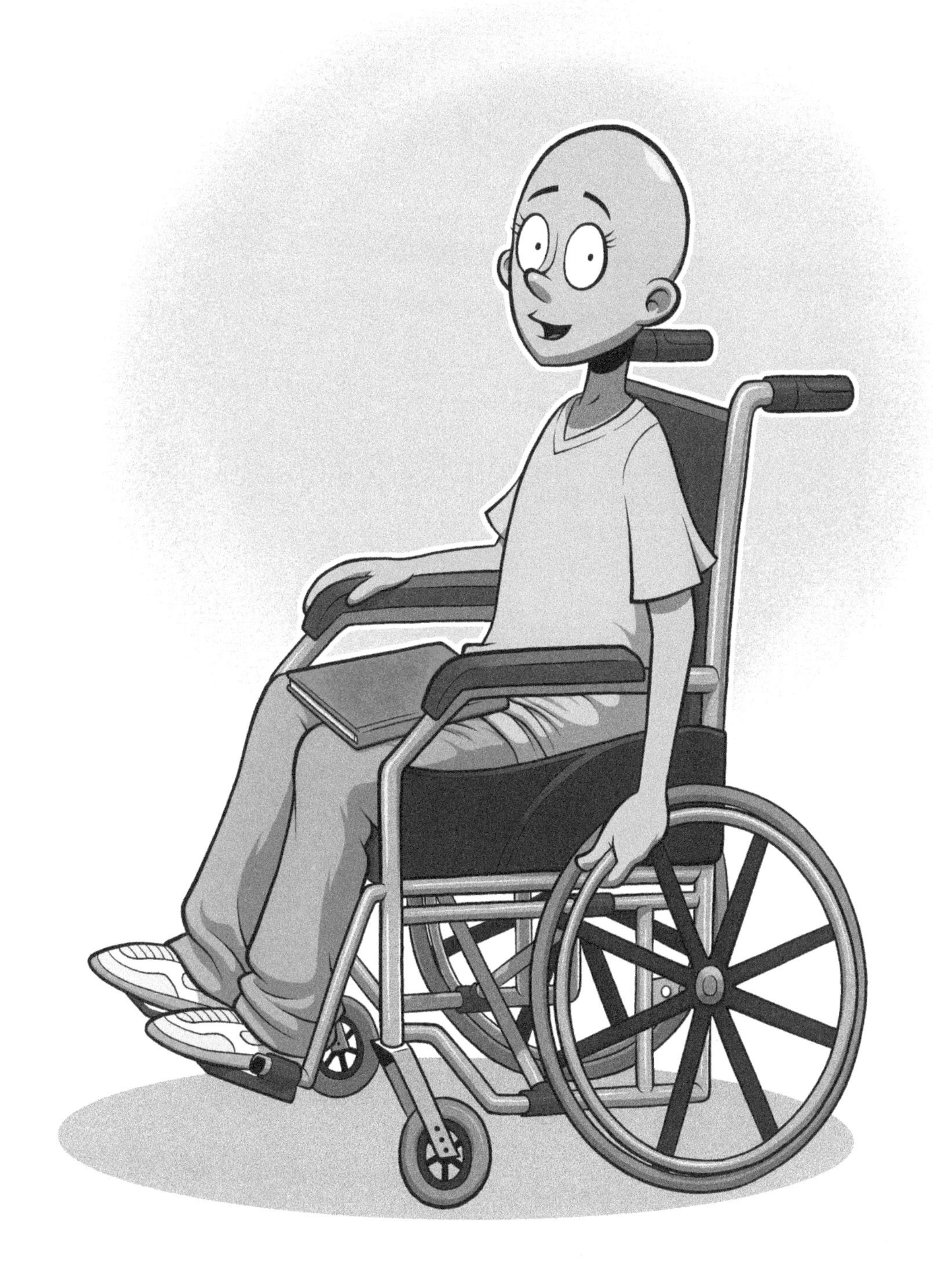

It's a pleasure to meet you--I'm Lucy. I'm in the hospital receiving my third round of medicine called chemo to fight my Cancer. For me, writing is a way for me to express how I'm feeling. It's too risky for me to go to school because this increases my chance of getting a cold or a flu, at a time when my body isn't strong enough to fight off these germs. Writing helps me fill the lonely times. But then, I can skype in the classroom to keep up with my studies and e-mail my teachers and friends!

Once you become **creative**, guess what?

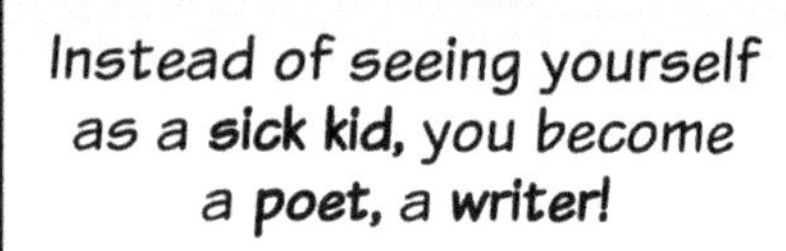

Poem:

If I was a shoe, where would I be?

Would I be in a hamper, or maybe a teepee?

Would my laces be tied, tangled, or torn?

Would my sole have cracks, would my soul be worn?

And if you find me, and I do stink,

Don't blame my owner, blame his feet

The **power of the pen!**

Journal your hospital **experience** by keeping a **diary or scrapbook.**

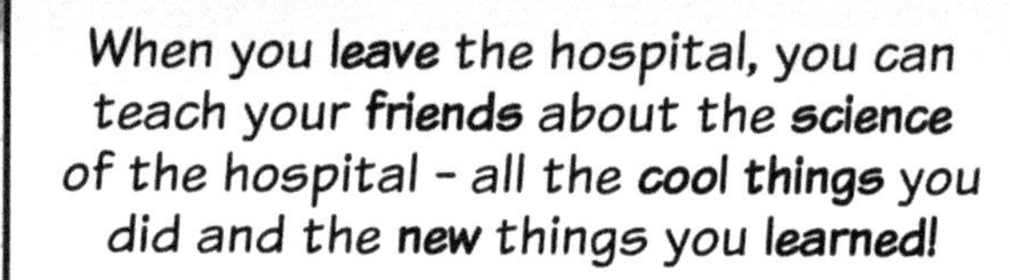

Write a mini book. It doesn't have to be chapters long - just a record of thoughts, feelings and photos if you want.
Draft 1
Let your mind wander the horizon!
Meet Jackson. He's autistic, and probably one of the smartest kids I know.
His mind and his senses are fine-tuned like a sports car - racing with ideas and revved up!
He's here because of seizures and when he's on a video EEG (a machine that picks up brain waves) he's stuck in his hospital room.
He makes the best of it with his creative thinking!
Even without pen and paper, there's always your imagination!

Illness is like a thunderstorm where the rain is made of tears.
You want the illness to end because it keeps you from feeling safe.
All you really want is to go home and not be sick anymore.

But you have to stay until you're stronger. So you find ways to cope.
Your interests keep you afloat as you discover a children's library inside
the hospital walls. Helping you to rise and float is **Angie's Place.**

HEY!
Wait - I found my missing shoe!
Thanks for the lift, Angie!
Keep a little courage in your pocket to get through your hospital days!...

In 1989, a golf tournament began…

"...Year one it was called the Cystic Fibrosis Tournament... then the Toledo Children's Hospital Tournament... then Angie's Place Pro Am. We always felt the name wasn't as important as the fact that money raised was helping kids.

The goal: to provide an endowment to ensure that Angie's Place will be at Toledo Children's Hospital... to help kids who are hospitalized... the seven year old who uses the computer, reads a book, listens to an audio book, or watches a puppet show has a better hospital experience because of Angie's Place.

...Golf can be rewarding. No matter how any of us play... we are helping some kids who have a problem get the best stimulation while receiving the best medical care at a state of the art hospital... in Angie's Place."

With Love to all the hospitalized children,
Dick and Alliene Liden (Angie's mom and dad)

I've been reading about how to grow giant pumpkins after I finish with my physical therapy for the day, even planted a seed in a pot and placed it on the windowsill of my room. Then transplanted it at home. I raised a 111 pound pumpkin! Pumpkins are like hope. You believe in the seed and it grows. My friends, my neighbors all planted pumpkins of hope for me after my stroke, and I was made an honorary FFA, Future Farmer of America, by my teacher at High School.

Hi. I'm Lacey. I have Cystic Fibrosis and a PICC line. Angie had Cystic Fibrosis, like me. A PICC line is tubing placed in a vein for medicine that can also be used to take blood samples for lab tests so I don't have to be poked every time a test is ordered. My PICC line has a bandage called a dressing over my skin that needs to be changed every so often. I need to keep this clean - so clean that you cannot even breathe on it - when the protective dressing comes off while the new one is applied to my skin. When my mom holds a book for me, I can look away and read it out loud to entertain my mom, the nurse and myself!

STORY-TIME
SELF-HELP BOOKS
AUDIO BOOKS
JOURNAL WRITING

COMPUTERS
HOMEWORK
PUPPET THEATRE
PAWS PROGRAM

Everyone knows you should keep a little courage in your pocket at all times. But what else is in there?

Want to play a game? Put one of the following things in your pocket, and tell someone they have three guesses which one is in your pocket! Or… ask someone to put one of these things in their pocket, and you get three guesses!

Aug. 24, '81
4 years old

Angie has been "reading" **We're on Your Side, Charlie Brown** by Charles Schulz.

One morning while I was washing her long hair, she started to cry. "Don't cry, Angie. Don't cry," I said.

"Don't cry? And deprive myself of an emotional outlet?" She answered.

We both laughed and laughed.

About Angie

Angie's Place was established at Toledo Children's Hospital by Richard and Alliene Liden in memory of their daughter Angela, who was frequently hospitalized with Cystic Fibrosis and passed away when she was six and a half.

Her love of reading gave her happy diversion from the world of CF and its treatment. At the suggestion of her pediatric pulmonologist, Dr. Pierre Vauthy, memorial monies were used to create this library for hospitalized children.

About the Illustrator

Isaac Klunk studied illustration and sequential art at the Savannah College of Art and Design before graduating in 2008. Now residing in Toledo, Ohio, he works as an illustrator, cartoonist, and caricaturist. His favorite animals are Tigers and Cicadas.

About the Author

To visualize this endeavor, **Kate Schwan** collaborated with her son Erik, who holds a BFA from Florida Atlantic University, Boca Raton. He resides in Sarasota.

The Clinical Coordinator of the Child Life Department at ProMedica Toledo Children's Hospital and a certified Child Life Specialist, Kate earned a certification in Rehab Counseling, as well as a masters degree from Bowling Green State University.

Kate lives with her husband, Mark Langenderfer, in Grand Rapids, Ohio.

CPSIA information can be obtained
at www.ICGtesting.com
Printed in the USA
LVHW071517041021
699489LV00006B/285